Word Revolt

Todd Rykaczewski

Be Kind

www.wordrevolt.com

ACKNOWLEDGMENTS

To the birds and trees in my life.

Contents

Ch.1   Metropolis   Pg. 1

Ch.2   Revolt   Pg. 27

Ch.3   Luv   Pg. 52

Ch.4   AEIOU   Pg. 68

Ch.5   THURIFER   Pg. 87

Ch.6   Plays   Pg. 106

CH. 1 METROPOLIS

City Lullaby

When the apple falls from the American tree
The death shall not bother me
For even the color of love
Is mocked by the black and white stars above
Can you hear the cry?
Of life in the city lullaby
Souls in chains
Marked by the tattooed to show the sane
Every time the second hand clicks
The shadow revile another trick
To keep its occupants on edge
Or hanging off the golden gate ledge
Never in a time of peace
Until the gears of the clock the minute's hands
released
Let the sky scrapers go down in size
Till the population has neighborly ties
As coupled loved walks the streets
Not fearing the thoughts connected to stranger's feet
Rows of dreams line the town
A place organized kids can be found
Simply quaint
Can you hear the cry?
City lullaby
An easy place to grow and faint
Then again there is that chime
Reminding the body to tell the mind about the time

Glass forms back into sand
Allowing the movement of the hour hand
To fertile ground
Of little chaos echo sound
When residing in a vast space
Well farmed with food it's laced
Far away from a crowded tone
Left with my mind to be alone
From an extreme of masses
To a lifetime never passes
Barren and stripped
A world transformed and flipped
I find the sky my only friend
Taking what I need never on lend
Can you hear the cry?
Of the city lullaby

Don't Give Up On Bailey

Her tremors start
With the evil queen freed
Addiction tokes the last bit of control
Her temporary fag light is smothered
Just short from being peaceful
On surveillance
That perfectly manicured face
Not to mention personality
Once again slips into the streets
With open arms curbed fingers welcome
Once more
The beaten voice ask through her eyes
Please
Is there anything I can do?
Generic voice of a trained mind responds
I'm sorry your prescription is refill too soon
Alone
Shaking
Her arms warped around her thin existence
Tears
You MOTHER FUCKERS don't understand!
Explains her soul as it turns black
Allowing her hope and progress to duel
Killing each other
As the young mind finds that perfect fit
That piece of skin still soft enough for a needle
Bailey

Broke
Allowing just enough rejection
Disappointment into her heart
To kill
Dying in the abandoned yellow house
Just down the street
From the pharmacy
Our child
Goes blue

World Market

Mother knitted
I looked for food
Shelter
Then a personal four year reproduction plan
Slowly showing my age
As my breed evolved becoming lazy
No longer surviving off instinct
Rather planning for the future
That later time past hungry
Further than genetics
Worlds torn from survival opening to verse
Revolving the moment you realize we have fallen
To our Knees
Converting
As American made tear gas fights the rest of the world
Here
Blindly fed ideas of progress are caned in china
Shipped to US
Like cancer
Gays
Most politics
The arts
Music
Yes even poems
Have fallen to nightly news
Current events never speaking of string theory
Equal event to written word

When power goes out
Allowing the one percent
Complete power
Over women
Man
Child
Our world
Known as the 99 percent
That is US

Wine In The Dark

Warm night and candle light
To my thoughts I try and say goodnight
Still your presence wins my peaceful right
As your words start the fight
Trying to close my past eyes tight
After all I'm just a man stuck with moral might
With humble height of my desire's sight
I wish the power would return and give me my light

Dead People Should Vote

I lost something today
That the government could not regulate
Or deem unstable
For society
And no angels of mercy
Could heal this emotion
Already well medicated
The fight is already won
When laws are created
Just to be broken
Or misplaced
But do I follow the dove
And fight to end human suffering
Or take a knee
To the judge
And slime my neck
Out of the hands of the prosecutor
Justified stolen meditation
Charged with malpractice
I fight for realism
Losing my state

There Is No Anchor To My Reason

Mad skies fire this treason
To ancient tap dancers on my ancestor's warship
For their amplification in the firing of souls
Is the very reason my sword may slip
Finding hearts at the end of my grip
An amulet at cores tip
Now you strive towards prejudice and confusion
And maybe mad
After all your education was served filet of sole
amandine
And nuts are only ok with legal execution
Just to prove how death is all awry
No matter rags, crown, or tie
We all share the human eye
Can you not see the amaranth on the grave?
Spawning pain
To rant and to rave
Is the alley cat not all American?
Worth the save
Resting our heroes in the cemetery named
A Pleasant Hill for the brave

Tea

As I lay in this tub
Floating in my own filth
That I managed to collect today
I find
That I'm a lazy man
Surrounded by my own
Dirt
Never willing
To take the time
And stand
Stand to wash this crud
From my fat body
To the tarnished grate
So far
From my head
To the drain
And right there it all starts
My own troubles
Washed away to join others
Of the same make
And model
To collect in a tub of melted mixing
Soup
I lay there till the water turns cold
Then I leave the tub to
Evaporate

Stranger Hall

Cranking the music box
I feel less silly in my emotions
Telling myself
This is a first for
Up until now
"Luv"
Was for a reason
Rather be
Committed relationship
Of just lust of skin
So no
Because I'm in some state
Related to when arrogance is involved
That pumps blood to my brain
Giving my mind power to decide
If clay only dried independently
A furnace
To place forever into a shape
This person
Only by photo
Never in bones
Is now their girl
I could watch die
Or madly unwind
Play a note or two
Then stop
As to say the reason the music
Ended

Was because you did not wind me up enough
To play forever

Arthritis

I've lost grip
As the tip of my finger and paper
Wages war
With the north penetrating
The South's virginity
Birthing change
To the now east
As many rags are used
In effort to dry the child
From holy water
Into this time
So simply
The working poor

She Was Much Taller Than Me

I took a cab to my friend's winter wedding
I guess because it was outside of my consistency
Realizing all I wanted to do is eat three AM cake
It hit
We let our minds get fat so our bodies followed
Focusing back it's asked
Sweet Sherry do you hear me?
Ring from our cups of tea
Realizing it's a coffee mug resting on her framed
Picture
The time for morning the consumption of treats ended
When the table cloth disappeared and cup rings
Appeared
No need for table settings over cherry oak
Placement begins
Ends with me and my daily strength
That ability to fight
What little pain I hold
When asked to dance by todays date
Kissing and swaying
Until the drums stop
Allowing my heart a chance for a solo
Beating out self-forgiveness
Excuses
Even pity and blues
Just because the ride I took from ancestral hues

Father Works On Trains

A man
Nothing like the wired
Modern mule
His hands have known steel
Grease
Cut skin and blood
Never beer
Just whiskey and true Gilded muscle
That soul
Who has from the time of cowboys
Followed tradition
Among the hard working grit
Dad
And his crew moves
China
Korea
Vietnam
India
Right through our corn fields
Soy beans
The land US
You and I
Hope proudly to pass to our kin
Fertile
Providing food
Protecting the boot wearing life
This country

Makes worth fighting for
So where the hell are our unity people
Our back bone?
Blue, red, and white pride
This land after all is our land
Remove that eye patch and see
That this mixing pot has gone cold
This sup needs to heat up!
And all the chicken and vegetables
Must
Start standing
And show
True Beef!

Tiffany

A stranger
As much so as the contents of sand
Standing at tides mark
Back turned to the sun set
Showing only a silhouette of beauty
As if the shade of black for a moment
Knew luv
Once again breaking a part all the colors
That are now all tainted and absorbed
When reality that the sparkle on the beach
Cuts your foot
By the broken home of a seashell
Just after the rocks kink your ankle
Finally taking rest on drift wood
The night redeems view showing only stars
Erie Island
Goes silent
Calm
Then dead
When no matter how much you wish for sight
Inland
Is just too far over the curve of the earth
Where never upon a time
Has already
To meet theirs
Just before untying a sinking sailboat
Kicking it into the waters direction
And if only once
Looking back at the stranded

The Next Earthquake Will Chip Your Parents Tooth

I don't want your vote
Nor your pity or luv
Your words should be brutal to my outline leaving
posture half colored
I want you to treat me nakedly mean metaphysically
speaking
Never glorifying blame in consumption of truth
Mutating the worlds wise production of moments in
production
Requiring torture of the merciful person
Left shooting up stuff into their homes
Right until the ordained level finds the floor
Wishing that nature never bought its poison from an
elevator
Realizing just how far a species will take abuse
Level one starts
As our morals shook once more
Leaving the human race under the framed door
Crying as the women's foundation melts
Dripping black and flesh tone make up all over
university's degrees
For once giving education a personal touch
After all this body is property to me not material
wealth and politicians
I ask myself to never foreclose on the banks
After all we our killing the earth
As she shakes
Bringing us to level two

As elder trees need to die so saplings can live
Luv must be forfeited for plastic so dirt not women
become fertilized
People need an expiration date
Or we will land on level three

As If The Coal Or Fate Had Meaning

I etched out my dreams on a broken seashell
Proclaiming the day fit enough
Spending decisions on the beach
Losing hope on shooting stars of past
Now traded in for a wishing rock
Skipped into the ocean
With the passing of the sail boats
Leaving me to wonder
If the water is any happier than the sand
Losing sight of the seagull stuck in the wind
I can't help
Watch the island sink into the sun
Releasing another day to be lost on shore
Reflected innocently by the floating dead fish
With only its broken body and intruding smell left to
the living
Crash
And the tide lands at my feet
To warn me of the time
Hinting with each wave
That my current position in life
Is no longer what it used to be
Proving just that
With each piece of tree that dies
Wood is reborn as driftwood
But aren't we all just floating around?
Through storms

Drying in the sun
Hoping someday to
Land
On a beach of our own

Shutting Down Plymouth

Ideal art sits in this crowded theater
Aged by the performances
Left by its artist
Now just scratches
Left engraved into the oak floor
As a painful memory
Or joyful display
A new lean
On an old idea
A performance
Shadowing the legends
In hopes to ride on their past words
Applause
And then the standing ovation
Cheering on the mirror reflection
Of a cherishing fan
Now an empty theater sits and listens
And dreams
Of the true
Who once were?
And now in lay
A generational groove
Never broken
The final curtain of swayed
And then
Silence

Notes:

Ch. 2 Revolt

Massive Amounts Of Candles

Shaken virgins
A candle burns with no flame to melt the time
Of the black days that shine onto the rest
Still the ants build their mansions
And birds fly in circles
With the spinning of the planets
The candle burns with a flame of water
And a young girl stands
Still as the earth rotates around
Trees growing in patterns
And every rain drop takes a number
Hide from the sun who likes to kill
Kill the grass that likes to shine
A candle flows through my head
Spiral with the pattern of the beat of my mind
Close the shutters to see the truth
Open eyes that see in a guided direction
Thoughts travel like a radio into nothing
Images of flight warp the picture frames
A candle that guide others
Fist of emotion flow with the wind
A flower cries toward the red sun
Young people injected by the flag
Clouds that shape squares
Time melts into my hand
Candles of brass that tarnishes

Reporters that report the night
Teachers beating drums to dictionaries
Faces of fire just seem cold
Rose to be blank
Twisted thoughts damper the candle
A bolder sits and thinks
Bridges that hold no weight
A mirror that reflects invisible common sense
The candle dies
Lights blind the virgin people

Unprotected Sex With The Government

Waiting for my thoughts to graduate
China
Peels the skin off American children
US
Becomes nothing but bone
Reflecting the economy
Our blood factories walk away
Hitchhiking on pollution
The corporation
Snuffs the burning bush
And the green dream
Only a hickey in place of a wedding ring
Then again
When a debt is due
Nuclear payment points to the throat
Neglecting the rest of the body
Quietly being bought
Turning freedom soil
Into cancer
Guiding the foreign pendulum
To separate the fat from the gravy
Like the constitution from the people
Supporting corruption
Allowing legally a business to be a person
Just without a soul or heart
The new global empire
Stands
Ready to fall

American Flags And Sad Sands

I'm standing still in this constant drip of time
As I watch broken glass plummets to the floor
The sight of eyes shine blank
Seeing the cracking white wall behind me
The windows of truth only send a glare
With the focus on the barren trees
A shout of my whispers travels the room
Into the shredding air
As it evaporates into the world of nothing
Only to be seen in the light
Till it floats into the shadows
Only to suffer the direction of the air
And with that
Stone statues melt from high blood pressure
Watching the people
As just a thought
That never comes into anyone's mind
Reflecting images with no distortions
Just as the moon never meets the hills
I wish I was a fish instead of a bird
It's hard to fly with nothing around
But to be supported by the ocean
Must be love
And in the end
I stamp out another day
Sitting and wondering about the blue sun
Just to hit the skip button

Cold feet hit the cement
As I take off into nothing
Trying to reach a certain black destination
From the start
I wish this day was not so heavy

Burning Oil

The cartoon cloth lies like a Mexican blanket
Providing structure
Between the American weed
No matter the thunder those rings provide
Simplicity will always have its bamboo lamps
As the green brass child sings
Never understating freedom or its wings
Paper lines the textbooks that play our kings
If only man
New god and their themes
Lucifer known as time
May never see your own luv over a string
Along the night the doorbell rings
The youth named mission sits on spring
Dreading fall and winters dream

The Weapon To End All Wars

My ancestors made church bells
Then his brother
Created bronze and industry
In terms
Forming our fathers factories
Better equipped
Building cannons
In shape of sound
Casted in weight to fire
God's noise became a gun conquest
Proving violence
Alive and well in the bible
And human nature
Taxiing us here
In our time of greed
Just in code known as stuff
Or any wealthy inscription of this economy
To our cashier Tele
Always dreaming of long distance
Operating his name diligently
According to the roads
Regardless the inventions
What once race felt now society sees
The pendulum swings
Just above a rope's presentment
As slaves to labor in the past
Live stuck in confinement

Known as medication
Giving the pharmaceutical gangs
Land ownership over Americans
Worse
Our world
A simple theater on the lecture lobotomy
Like priest and doctors
Those with intentions of the modern time
Believing they know best

Uniforms

It starts with a child
And grows to an adult with a thought
Even though you can't kill a story
You can replace one
With clothing that looks alike
I never saw it coming
The day I traded this in
For your idea
To abandon my every
Passion
And unplug the colored water
So I could see the top
Of matters
So it
Starts with my decision
And ends far from your own
Sunscreen from a coming storm
Keeps you from every
Feeling the rain
Or to understand the wind
You stand there
Learning the ways of
Your ancestor's youth
And searching for America
Only to find it's impossible
Due to the string you
Follow

Cheap Entertainment

Be soft
And luv me still
Your actions may be quiet
Then I see your innocence
Like a gnat around thought
That fly full of distraction
Pulling truth like unkempt sails
Towards unfriendly winds
Until tainted water fermented in oats and age
Drowns the red blood cells
Those other words would have saved
Informing that yes
This decision
That the sole of your feet
Are about to commit
Maybe foolish
Ignorant
Downright stupid
Just to follow the motion of the now
We should cry
Not laugh
For the speed we travel
Stimulates our minds was past detail
As the simplicity
Known as beauty
Grace

Charm
Power and decay
Even true luv has past right by
Never seeing through the lights confusion
Projected by instant gratification
The need for cheap sunglasses
Has never been more important

Presidents Fear

Long live the dead king
Torn from his spot in the ground
And robed from his riches
Filling in the hole he once covered
Cries of joy as you tear down the reason
You stood your ground
And replace the values grey mold
Growing on the broken stone
Among your feet
Just for you to rebuild your thoughts
Cement of time cracks
As children in uniforms walk the line
Don't fear your mind forming a puzzle
Leafs flow down stream
But trees grow into the sky
Standing in the wind
But breaking during storms
The pink grass grow invisibly
And the green showing with all its glory
As a jester laughs at a pattern
A baby cries of disapproval of its birth
Poured into a mold
Then stamp with the animal slogan
Improvement of death only proves negative
As spring brings snow
Crows hold their head high
Till the sun rises blocking the truth
And the night frees

Can't Own A Photographer (M.J.B.)

Why is it on the face of time
Great empires build temples for the ones they luv
On the left lie lands of paradise
The right house of the masses
Center of course the court
Playing nervously with the egg in their pocket
Full of opium ready to be mixed with memories tea
Hallucinating on the symbols
Laughing at the general public
As long as the secret texts played spiritual agreement
To oceans cause
Prickling the back of public mood
The mounted elephant looks less horrified
To those cooking
Alive and stuck in prison
Well at least a head on a table behind bars
Left as a quest
Dissatisfied as a local war
Proving wonderland
Has yet created
a composers versioned companion
Discovery of her femininity program
Makes me wonder about soul
A simple energy
Lost

Smallest Things Can Kill

You created me
Torched and twisted
Drugged through life
Nothing more than an outcast
Thieving from hearts
Hidden behind theater's mask
Portraying those traits
No powdered soul could change
Just a product of ideas
As thunder rolls off the producer's tongue
Masters creation of manipulation
Must live on
Echoing off into memory
With the peoples storm just arriving
First drops of pollution
Landing tempted on my forehead
Pushing the filth into my eyes
Until the truth reaches my lips
Salty lies
Slip back into my open mouth
Lightning strikes
Shaking the posed shelters
Only angering me
Here I am!
On my bones as you wished
Kill me
Or let me live

Not by the hour of postponement
Finding what is seen
When eyes closed Unbearable
Never to be a freed slave
When days reek of shadows
Casted by the very tune of your whistle
End this trial I demand it!
Thunder roles
Masters creation of manipulation
Must live on
Then why bring this onto earth!!?
Showing the already vain
With shame
Strike me dead!
Or leave me still
But don't leave me linger
In old James Mill

White People Luv To Cut Down Trees

A leaf falls into a puddle
After a long slow glide
In the wind
And as green as the day it grew
It lies and admits water ridges
Disturbing
The Peaceful calm
Of everything
It never falls again
But sits
And with every sunny day
Grows old
Yellowish
Brown
And when the puddle dries
The leaf dies
Cracking
Then
Dust
Not in the wind
That's to conventional
But into soil
That melts into the drain
During a moonfish storm
And that little green leaf
Is used for sewage
To clean my waste

Press Cancel To Continue

Paint peeled off the window sell
Chipped exclusions
Of white wash conclusion
Explaining the lead pride
Gathering under the glass
As I find the piano impulse
Traveling past the frame
With the pig
Through the door
Only one choice remains
The picking of that bow
To be worn to the ball
If only for the night
Charmed
Honored in dance
Turning around on a floor
Is most
Invigorating
Far from question
Who really is fortunate?
To have
Happy manners
In courtship and appearance encouraged
With statue
A short man alone smelling a weed
Desired audience being with the man
Quality and torment
Mistaken as suspended policies

This accord
Is
Declined

Dreaming Into Hands

Nothing
like the wealth's favor of gravity's high drama
Wisely delivering the hand over details
Overlooking the down
No
Not onto the movement of colored flower pots
Stuck
Illustrated by natural pigments
Derived from yellows
To clear
Into this place
Of sources and watercolors
Known shaded by belief
Yours
To fast or slow no matter location
The leader gets to drink
First
That's what I thought
The day to day
Auctioneering modern to corner side walls
Our powerful laugh
Purpose
Care in chalk walk
When living in portraying
Regardless of hues
Or
Grey hair
Threatens to continue
Relearning over balding practice

Pushing villages mute
Leaving perception in clean air
Till they say please
Talk

Finding Peace

I found a thought today
Lynched
And hanging from a tree
A wooden sign warned me
Burnt words
This sign was once a part
Of this tree until the branch grew
Eastern in this humble south town
I thought for a while
Looking at the half of tree
That could only shade me from the south
Placing my hand on its rotting bark
Storing a piece in my pocket
As a gift of remembrance
If my journey north
Ever became unbearable
I would know
Where I came from

An Auspicious November

Every influence
Continues to write chapters
Long after the leaves fall
Even when all the venters take their final trip
Lose color
We are left with the crisp reminders of law and birth
Leaving the days to decompose our seasons
Voluntarily reminding us where we formed
A simple perfume that lies on the flesh of time
Holding each individual bottle
Up to the retailed light
So you can see the portrait through seemed glass
Continually
Playing out the exact moment that scent was mixed
Explaining how that person moved through the air
As if it was head or ambrosial
Fumed and fragrant
Aromatic floating on the edge of malodorous
A temporary perception on how they were judged
Always interacting with personal soil
That later birth plants
Used in creating unique aromas
Forming a liquid stamp over enveloped clothing
Announcing to the world its worth and timeline
Inked
With a self-representation on how we want
Packaged
Labeled
Sprayed with DNA

Then filled with a letter
Full of words by those we hold
Just like the leaves under the Blue Spruce
Providing what little is left
From fallen brown forms of concentrated life
In hopes
The air will smell like pine

Notes:

Now blog: www.wordrevolt.com

CH. 3 Luv

Ridge Road

A rose floats along in the rain
Washed away by the sorrow of a broken heart
A young girl stands
Alone
On the curb
Looking into the sky
Watching
As each rain drop gathers with her tears
Melting her soul
Each drop taking from what little is left
Pain rushers through her every bone
Her mind swirls with agony
Each strike of lighting
Bringing back a picture of her
Love
Burning into her eyes
Then as fast as they came
All goes dark
A cold wind blows past her body
Goose bumps run up and down her legs
Like the end of summer
Or the last leaf to fall from the tree
Reality starts to overwhelm her thoughts
She shrills
But no sound is made
Cries
But not words flow
All that's left
Is her standing
In a black and white world
Rain flows

And tears overcome
The beauty and elegance
Of a once loved woman
Alone
In the dark
With only a word
Once blossoming and full of life
Now dark and rotten a way
A word that was never
Spoken
A word that was never
Heard
A word that died
With the happiness of a young woman
A signal word
That was never
Said
So never
Happened
Left on the corner
In the rain
As a tear flows from her eye
To her cheek
Into nothing
Alone
With that word
Never heard
Luv

Political Funny Paper

Aiming my Astrolabe across their soul
I found flesh throwing off luv
As my professors sat in their athenaeums
Proclaiming human body conditions were to blame
Providing the stimulated skin as proof
To the azure in our eyes
Never minding Augur standing on his best work
Looking over my cuzin
From the 2nd or 8th marriage
Who
Enjoys proclaiming
Their bisexual ability to tell the future
Simply by observing the flight patterns of birds
Announcing union in thought
Not gratification allowing
Success to form possession in perverse union
Just between releasing stress and meaning
This person falls for my coquetry
An act over thrifting conversation
Focusing on the copestone to be placed
Finishing off our grave situation

Crystal

I need to rent a costume
I fear this skin no longer fits
It was that cute boyish blue or girlish pink drag
Your parents put on you
Telling you how to wear it right
 Protected from all the school events
As they smoke their fags
Never understanding that a you don't pick identities
They pick you
Regardless
I slip off that scratchy cotton made in Vietnam skin
Doing my part as to give it to good will
Like some poor soul
Would want to go through the world
Looking as I did then
But now
Oh now I went to the magical farm and got refitted
Ah yes an entire new world
For now I am me
Not that rent a disguise
That covered this kid so long
I may go to the winery and talk poetry
I may sip on coffee and fight philosophy
Maybe even luv you
The person I could not love before
In my old skin
Yes
I may even luv you

Be in luv with u
And when asked
Share my luv for you
I was made capable to choose the disguise
Of my liking
The perfect one to hide behind
Or flaunt
For now I am as you will be
For when you take that mask off
And see
We are modern luvers
You and me

Road Kill

The flowering weed proves its evidence
Towards the pollution all summer long
Then betrayed by the weeds very creator
As winters death moves in
Ignorantly
Providing the process all love follows in nature
Just as the powered blue sky turns coal black
Your eyes into my soul but then never look
Back
Just in time for the seasons to tide
The chill in the air ends the warmth between our lips
For us this may not have been forever love
Still we have those nights we loved
Relating fate as a child and our time
With the picked flower
Knowing our happiness
Could only live so long in a vase on the table
Finding comfort in the idea our friendship
Was beautiful
Enough to be a center in our individual lives
Leaving the memory of what was
Edged and shrined by the earthy barren spot
The garden
Letting those who will later come know
There once was something there before them
A time when the sun shined
The soil was fertile

And just for a season
You felt
Complete

Still About You

When our birds fall from grace
The ballerinas' morgue will not be made a play
Musical
Or even opera
For the cello
Piano
Hopeful violin
Will not have the tune playable to the pain or joy
The conductor of life requires
As he twist the tired wires
Manipulating steel along with wood
Skin and talent
Not forgetting to insult the blisters
Blood
And time
Setting talent alongside of luv and passion
Breading those raised and taught
That soul
Is like playing music
The more it hurts
The better it sounds

Repressive Camps Over Digital Expression

My heart keeps going because my parents need it to
Truth
It stopped when I lost you
Yes there is nothing like losing a child
Yet after years my luv is far from wild
As if it was then
Is now
Pain
I love you
No matter the balance
Modern list
Has an exception of crime
Trusting decades in the ability to jail
Ambitious guitar chords
Played
One at a time
Never politically dissembling war crimes
On their own terms
Trusting old men
They become elite solders of the wheel of justice
An extreme of tools
Duty bound in frustration
Disappointing principles
Wishing people would survive in vengeance
Framed in decades
Threatening youths
Families
A little boy
So if you're young

A moment in a girl's life
The belt
Holding our pants up to say
"God be with you"
Nothing less than a suicidal note to pride
Waiting 100 years to the arrest
Showing organization as details
Ignoring bread
Yet to prove rations
To those believing
Right
Those in red white and blue
And experience in genocide
Records in testimony
Self-preserving the case we all see as self-salvation
Voting this system
Motivational

Cara

I can still taste the ash from her smoky kiss
Lacing my words with her existence
Proclaiming myself
As hers
Forcing my wandering mind back
Into friendly conversation
Sipping on the first comfort cup of coffee
Finding foreign word dull
Sensing the fall of senses
Her smell lingers from some part of my body
Like a scar from a forgotten reminder
Or string around my finger
One can't help
But slip
Neglecting sound as just a vibe
Commandeered by everything not seen on the dark
Shading out the now
Letting distant company respond
Off the echo of their own words
Limping
Focus is found redeemed by my fifth drink
Now more than ever a gulp than a sip
With sight slipping into intrusive images
Her body nude with just a beaded necklace
Again out time intrudes on the hour of reasonability
For as I leave
I poor this cup of coffee black

Flowers For A Stranger

Framed by fate
The unforgiving sun leaks through
A well faded window
Temporarily illuminating the dust
Caught on a journey
From unnoticed
Into perspective
Eventually collecting together
Distributed evenly
Over my journal
Slowly fading
Even my most private thoughts
As desire fades
Into friends
And this feeling evolves
Into something more
In reflection
To nothing at all
Yet
Just yesterday afternoon
I could see so wide
And love so far
Now
My only stand
Is my personal revolution
Towards my guilt
Contentment

And the reason
Today

The Help

A lady in waiting
Sits and stairs at her queen
As she feels the dress with love
That she will never wear
A feeling of resentment
This lady shall bear
As this queen of riches
Sits in her grand chair
Only the secret I know
About her balding head
Makes for an even trade
And all is fair
But still I kiss the ground
This queen walks on
As I only feel anger
Not pride
My day shall come
As all days do
That she will only
Be able to ask who
For I will be standing
Above her
For I am the lady in waiting
And as for now
I serve
Waiting
Till I'm the lady in morning

Child Care

A cry of a childless confession
Echoes these empty halls
The absence of a
Mother
Refuses to answer
Alone and on her own
She learns to
Stand
Black and white
A young girl learns to hate the world
Trust into suspension
Born a rebel
Standing in the rain
Those legs to thin for her burden
Love that she could not show
Hidden by a smile she shares
Blocking her anger toward depression
No end to the beginning
No start to the new
Wisdom blocks crystal tears
Logic tattooed on everything
The hell becomes still
And a child learns not to
Cry
Dependent on herself
A new world through the eyes
Of the Youth

Experimental gratification

Like driftwood she was meant to be free
My crazy diamond far across the sea
Genetic luv from the leather to the tree
A page in the bible and origins of species to see
Is distance just not a fee
To my crazy lion far off in our salty tea
Offering her rusting marigold to me
Time drops
And he is she

Notes:

Now Blog: www.wordrevolt.com

CH. 4 AEIOU

If Jesus And Buddha Could Hold Hands

Two souls visited my door
A youth in search of something grand
And a elder
Surrounded in what she had found
In hopes of giving it away
Jehovah's witnesses
Trying to show me the light
If not
A book for all the people
To inspire some
Risk it all for the others
Be the reason for death to many
For the light is not always ours to see
And our way
Is just that
The trust in the bible
Finds its quilt in any liberty
In line for being used
Hung for mortality
Till what's left drying
Is profitable
Sparingly or materialistic
For the round table of today
Sits barren
The chairs broken
Left for free

Leaving us to walk this journey
Giddied by the philosophers of the past

Leader

At the halls end
Lays red
The color of a scarf
Hung
Door knobbed
A calling out
Of sorts
Leveling the playing field
Standing sideways
Becoming smaller
So my heart was not an easy target
To be shot
When dulled
This piled by a gun
Trading loyalty for lust
So honor expands
Past Alfa dog luv
Showing names
Titled
In the end
Posed
With song
Welder
Conductor
Old
On the cheap

Cheap Entertainment

Comments be soft
And luv me still
Your actions may be quiet
Then I see your innocence
Like a gnat around thought
That fly full of distraction
Pulling truth like unkept sails
Towards unfriendly winds
Until tainted water fermented in oats and age
Drowns the red blood cells
That other words would have saved
Informing that yes
This decision
That the sole of your feet are about to commit
Maybe foolish
Ignorant
Downright stupid
Just to follow the motion of the now
We should cry
Not laugh
For the speed we travel
Stimulates our minds way past detail
As the simplicity
Known as beauty
Grace
Charm
Power and decay

Even true luv
Has birthed right by
Never seeing through the lights confusion
Projected by instant gratification
Proving the need for cheap sunglasses
Has never been more important

The Bell Would Ring

Frightening the crow out of the tower
Before they could do real harm
As make nest
Leave feces
And have a chance to molt
Clogging the yesterday's church music
With black feathers
Stopping the trimly swing of tradition
That would allow more colorful birds
A place to make home
Cracking that bell
Known as liberty
Then I say let it crack
Fall from grace
Lose its high position above the people and God alike
Smashing to the ground to the tone of old rights
I would rather live in a world of silence
Then charm and ignorance
For the mistake was the killing of trees
The perfect perch
To those in need have rest
All in the name of erecting a building
That is forced a title
Laid in religion

One Subject

There he stood beached
A few feet from my sanity and the pushing tide
Tossing tiny lake shells into the water
Diseased with algae
Flick
Calm
Splash
Then his timid brown eyes looked over
Sounded with wrinkles and uncertainty
I could feel the wake
Each time the mighty wave broke
Emitting a tiny circle on conformity
As the light held on like a fish refusing to just float
Till reflection lost its stand on the white shell
The army green water was just to think
Flick
Calm
Splash
His wondering
Warn eyes once again searching over me
In almost to the same beat of his increasing breaths
His sight
Never resting
In one spot long enough to get caught
Then in a panic state
He moved closer
Tripping a little over his untied shoes

Finally
Catching his decaying body
Bringing it to some form of rest
Just feet
From my once solitude
No longer the sanctuary I had enjoyed
What had been smooth sand and warm air
A cool under tone
Now personal hell of aged stone and dead life
Now harshly shadowed by this intruder
Hunching over in his black cutoff jeans
Crying filthy shirt
His body just simply stained in laziness
Or maybe distraction
His very look spoke old and decrepit imagery
Just by his presence stagger
I almost for a moment felt compassion
Sorrow
Maybe even a little guilt for how I judge him
Until again
Flick
Calm
Splash
Then yet another crooked look over my body
Searching my existence for strength
But more important scouting for its flaws
He knew some part of me had to be weak
And that's where he would lay his attack
Into everything I knew understood
Ending my very fight for survival
Showing the world

With only my corps
I was not worth a burial at sea
Or even lake
That's why my remains were left here on this beach
Made of crushed stone and shell
Flick
Calm
Splash
Once more judging the area
On how he could leave me here
With the smoked cigarettes
Drift wood
And water soaked bones
Eventually being covered up and forgotten
A part of the shore
Flick
Calm
Splash
Now I could feel the wrenched heat
Stench from his body
For the stranger was right next to me
This thing reeking of colorless order
Letting a few shells fall out through dirty fingers
Keeping one
Flick
Calm
Splash
Slowly taking a long breath through my mouth
I stood
He smiled
We hesitated a few threads apart

Then as if age had not torn down onto him
Tearing his ability to move
This thing quickly
now with steady focus on my own
Reached into his pocket
Still showing his gums
Rotting teeth as to distract from his pending deed
No longer frail but swift in his actions
The only retched smell was his confidence
As his hand flew from his pocket
All I could see
Was the sun spot stains on the top of his hand
And something in his twisted arthritic fingers
Going right for my heart
Slam
Calm
Splash
His elderly body and the brick hit
Water at the same time
As so did the track
Titled
Are You Ready To Die?

God's Hands On Gays

A tear that flows from my eye
A single tear that just seems to mean so much
Yet
Has no effect at all
A tear with the power of the ocean
A tear that seems to smother the light
That burns inside
That kills the love once exploding with joy
Now just washed into the lake
Lost feelings forever
Expanding
Fueled by others
Who only have hate in their hearts and sorrow
Chaining to your feet
Keeping you from flying free in the wind of joy
Causing your heart to grow sad along with theirs
Forever trapping you at their level of sadness
Defeat
A tear that seems to transfer to tears
Sadness converts to pain
All the joy and love once felt toward others
Seems to dwindle into nothing
Space inside once where a heart jumped
To the beat of love
Soul sang along with the tone of joy
Now there is just a space that I forever fall into
As to free fall in a dark tunnel
With no idea of direction
No hope to see the light at the end

A tear caused by the look of pure hate into my eyes
Hate caused the evil that burns inside all of us
By the path chosen
Feeding into the hate
Giving a reason to let out the devil
That screams inside
I sit down and picture you gazing upon me as if
I were an outcast
The very reason why your life seems so dark
I see your heart
With so much anger
Your mind with so much pain
looking upon me as if it was my fault
You gaze upon me as to say you hate me
You gaze upon me to say you never want me around
I gaze on you as a tear flows down my cheek

Trading Bibles And Guns

Priest sits
With hair of gray
As his hat stretches for the sky
And his red velvet coat
Dripping to the floor
Behind
Sits a decorated general
Stern and strong
With his boots ever so perfect
Both sit in school
And learn
As the solider kisses his ring
Sins are forgiven
As a purple heart shines
Behind lays a thought
Of a boy
Neither priest not solider
A broken law
Unforgiving
He was laid into an eternal sleep
A priest and soldier
Sit in a row
Forgiving each other
Unforgiving

Bubble Bath

I sent my dreams into the air like a Sunday prayer
Sadly
The messenger was a bubble
Pop!

Hey Hey Old Age

I shook hands with the old man
Of my future
Who even in my dream
Reminded me to shake hands
With the right
Not left
It was freighting dream
Of a time that my youth
Will only be a dream
And every white lie
Will mock a lost hair on my balding head
And I
A grandparent
With only ghost as parents
Until my own white death
And my child has a dream
About shaking hands
With himself

Fool's Gold

My mother warned
Be aware of the preacher
For their twisted autobiography
May be the strive to be a teacher
As stone and brick creates the house of God
Without soul and mortar they are mere feature
Yet, what is stain glass to faith
But sand
Once touched by all gods holy hand
Who have empowered by doing
Not priest ridden swooning
After all our body without moral reason is a creature
My child I luv you
Be warned of the preacher
That person with a wicked tongue
Like an old rag there conscious hung
For when they see the holy light
Its hells fire reflecting there might
Sadly they could care less about us
Because the heart is cancered
With moneys lust
Now don't pass this off as a mothers nag
No matter the sown colors on your flag
And don't take this as a religious hook
For all God's people shall have their own book
Even if you don't have a faith to bare
These words are still yours to wear

So as you stand in life and listen
Be aware of the words that glisten
My child know your teacher
Live life through your own mind
And be warned of the preacher

Notes:

CH. 5 Thurifer

Personality Test

I killed a man once
Not with anger or revenge
Words were never spoken
Battle lines never drawn
Yet he died
But not by my fist honored
Or due to his mental state
Still he lay with no breath
And not because of passion or fear
Don't even think it was because I was desperate
You would be a fool to think so
One problem still lingers
The man dead in my pond
Funny really
Who dies in a pond?
But a man longing to quench
A thirst

Weekend Dreams

The Little boy lingers
In that charcoal penciled place
Better known as the timid night
And even though his voice is tickled in youth
The words are far from juvenile
As the nouns armor death
Defeating the painted rays of light
Leaving only his tiny shadow to be seen
As if black ink was dripped on white silk
Due to the pain of writing a good bye letter
Or conscious dancing on the mind
That just wants rest
Again timely words whisper
Though wind chimes and shadows
Just past old memories
Then right into the left ear
The child rehearses once more
Stain glass
In this church will never last
For the reaper of aberration knows your past
Stronger than your love and soul you hold fast
Until all other thoughts become barren and vast
This plaque will own you
At last
At last

Some People Suck As Teachers

A boy flicks a pebble in hopes to strike
Me
But not to cause pain
Or leave a little red mark upon my skin
No
In reality he flicks an emotion
That embarks on a journey
To set an inscription on my personality
And dissolve the writhes
Bringing forth the filtered
Corruption
Yet as he sits in confusion on bags of manure
Starring through plastic doors
Into the green house
He only finds my outline
Among a field of colors
Slowly fading away
At least from him
With consumption
Understanding
Or loss of interest
The pebble falls
Into the gravel which it came
Sadly outcaste in its new destination
For its assistance in a undesired motion
As for me

I've found no glory in this success
Only aroused
From the leach it formed
Setting dinner of seven
In the grand hull of my
Ship
Still to this day
The pebble sits
The boy a ghost
And I
Live humble and free in my existence

On The Roof Of China

I can't stand to stand
Or the thought of being alone
Anger goes through my mind
Fighting a war
I should not have to fight
Wrestling a monster
That all I want is love
In the end I will win
And enjoy the fact that I lost
So call the guards
The cops will never respond
To the death of this kind
To the death of a family
Town from the inside
By the pillar that holds it firm
click click
Then the time cracks
As it laughs upon my shadow
That fears the dark
And in the mist of all this
I hang my head
And cry

Walmart's Missing Child Of The Month

Ten years old a young girl runs with the glory of life
A breeze
Dances her hair forming around a soft face
The weight of time could not push her down
As she floats by
And her cloud of trust brings memories
To the old
And a smile to the youth
Most important
Love to her parents
Every sunny day can be just as cloudy
And every rain drop can bring hope
But life has its way
We all end the same
A cloud shifts over the sun
Baring no drops of hope
That young girl becomes
Breathless
Time shifted into the future
A man hits the lotto
Parents become widowed to the chilled
Stones of age cover a young girl
Into her fate she is punished
With nothing but darkness
Little tears flow from her eyes
A cry calmed by the truth of soil

Left alone
To face those monsters in the night
A cry for mom
A shriek for dad
The last beat of a small heart
Parents standing
Morning
An empty coffin
For their lost chilled
There lost life
Just alone with the guilt
Of being late
To pick up the broken tears
To their black eyed girl

Are You Safe On Birth Control?

Her eyes cried jade
As rhinestone ashed her heart
She once knew her existence
That time before recommended medication
And love
Well yes
She knew love like a child
Pure and full of innocence
At least as far as the mind goes
Yet the revolution
Between birth control and unprotected sex
Was mute
With only genetics and alcohol abuse to blame
Was it luv?
Does it matter?
Our world was better off because of it
Proving that neglecting those "things"
Labeled important in relationships
Are simply guesses
On what really creates matrimony
Like blinded gunfire
On death do us part

1,000 Oreo Jokes

A free man and all just after the harm
Finding surprise due to a warrants arrest
Giving law
The grounds in evolvement over feet as long as
human condition falls under the colored
But not those under God
But under liberty we stand
Crazed
Ready for reporting the very much
Honor
Extras will pay for in the universe
Microwaving the extinct until they rage
Showing teeth and trophies to our kids
Asking the hard question
Is this worth money or ammunition?
Well?
Are you impressed or ready to be shot
After all you're faced with human condition
Not humiliation

Friends Of Sort

A line is drawn between
Artist
And
Insanity
Both twisted into a passion
And tormented, hand fed
Plaque to the mind
But when does a painting
Become a voice in your head
And your own ear in the palm of your hand
To calm it down
Or when a writing
Finds you
And turns to reality
As your own heart beat drives you
Frozen drunk
Lying dead in a gutter
When does that white lie
No longer feel the space
And become a white death
When does art become your mind?
And your mind slips across the line

Generation Of Greed

I was lying in a cloud of thoughts
Just lost in the truth
All I could see seemed translucent
Then I fell into a dream
Just standing in my mind
Waiting for the ships to set sail
Into the world until
A tone pitches in my mind
Causing me to remember what
Was
It just seems to never end
Then again the sun has not yet set
Seems everybody has a smile
But I face this wall of rain
And force my trial
The things I could tell you
That would kill your innocents
But u seem to like your way
Forget about my twisted world
I wake
My eyes open into nothing
As my sight sinks into the day
Just another dream of another dead man
Being blind doesn't bring me down
It's only twisted thoughts that find me
And you will come around

18K

The moth finally hit the wall
Then as my little sister poked its wing
The magic dust fell off
Unable to fly
The bug became depressed
Then died on the floor
Quickly understanding humility

Nothing Means Nothing

Books and cardboard boxes
Have everything in common
Both made of paper
And hold the same thing
That being
Nothing
And when it rains
Its stiffness
Dissolves
Into its true form
Trash
Behold this concept
A book in a box
It's like a person in a person
A birth
Already written and published
From day
One
With no hopes of transformation
I can only hope
My lost interest
Is not my box's releasing rain
So at the end
I leave it to you
To drop this in the nearest puddle

The People's Garden

A seed into soil
Doesn't always make a plant
A seed into a woman
Doesn't always make a child
An idea into the mind
Doesn't always make an action
Passion into your eyes
Doesn't always create love
Denial of the truth
Doesn't always stop death
But it helps sometimes to water
Even if it's sand
And it works even better if it's
From your body
But we warned
A child could kill you
As well as a plant
And when the death is wanted
Only life will prevail
Junkyard love
Could be worse
And an idea
Could really just be
That
An idea
So only water those
That you want to water you

If Tuesday Happened

The lamp played blue
As the chair red
Fighting importance over the rug
Guarding the exit
Laid green and straw
Like the people through the door
Said stiff
And for the best walked all over
Creating lies
Making some rise from the cream to the fat
Landing others drowned
Unattached and hung over
Playing back to the oil monarchy
Sucking on the supply nipple
Blossoming the sands and east
To pay child support towards the states
Stuck in onesies
With a flap on the back
Allowing the shit to flow
As intended by nature
Selling the kid to slavery in attempts to free
You and me

Killing Tree

Kill the child
As a man walks from its remains
Into something
A time
A place
That may bring honor
Or a trip that will wear into nothing
And alone will he die
Will people standing all around
Thinking about everything
But him
I laugh upon them
Mock their ways
Nothing can stop this insane smile
As I look
Into the tears shredded by fogged glass
I see what I was blind to all along
Notice that small thing in life
The one thing never told
This journey starts with you
And ends
With them

For A Friend

I'm going to fall apart
As my kiss
Lands hearted
If only good together
Is where it started
Then we could drink paint
Find a night and know our saint
And in the am ask
Do you luv me?
Are my words truth
Can loneliness not feel my touch?
Understand my grip
If not
Then why are these eyes not your mirror?
If what we had was to a stranger not my dear
Just as a feather off road kill
Bleeds a tear
Killing Mermaid romance
Under fresh water so you never hear
With kids and solid roots in time
That age of responsibility equals fear
Even if sex
Laid in public
At its best
Including absorption
Chest to chest

Breast to breast
This organ is just not ready
For the test

My Power Ranger Is A Collectible

Just a plastic man
Stored in a box
Painted a forced color
Molded perfection
Permanent mask and all
Just waiting to be played with
Forced to fight evil
Armed with a child and a fake gun
Evil imagination stands no chance
If only it could move on its own
And this stigma
That it's an action figure
From some dated show
Stuck with a title
With a few adventures years
Then forgot about
Forever
Unless the attached popularity
Gives value
To be saved
Existing solely for others
Just a toy

Calculator

I wish that I was smart
So I could place an equation to my life
And calculate my out come
To a number I could understand
Related to my problem
Connected to my story
But there is no solution
To the equation
That I wonder
If time is not relevant
And dimensions are in our eyes
Then who is to say
The magic number
Time spent on writing
Is time gained in math?
An equation of words
That must equal a
Thought
A thought that
Transmits nothing more
Then this
A poet's equation
Mathematically imperfect

Burning Oil

The cartoon cloth lies like a Mexican blanket
Providing structure between the American weed
No matter the thunder those rings provide
Simplicity will always have its bamboo lamps
As the green brass child sings
Never understating freedom or its wings
Paper lines the textbooks that play our kings
If only man
New god and their themes
Lucifer known as time
May never see your own luv over a string
Along the night the doorbell rings
The youth named mission sits on spring
Dreading fall and winters dream

CH. 6 PLAYS

19 Raglen Street

Scene: After finishing his third drink Angelo can't help but start to think about last month, this time. All seemed as lost as it does now. If only the past could be replayed, then maybe Mariah Joe could help him stand on his courage and leave some reminder that his identity is not like pain. It will thrive no matter the sedative. Always, pushing past the tattoos and piercings and never noticing the correction of stature as the body lands in play. Showing how even if we act out every motion to fit in, we will always be that person stuck with our thoughts at night trying to fall asleep. Writing down our ideas in any form the limited light will allow, as long as our minds find peace. If not then a night of unrest, as Angelo finds himself, writing this poem on a piece of old mail.

Walking in, floating on whispers
Her dress hung in red only to be framed in black
Flowing over a well posed coat hanger used for years in dance
Walking such a way as to avoid the light but remain
Composed
As if flesh denied the days seeking to be transparent
Proving to the world how pure she was
Showing the lack of touch from the harshness of a luvers rage for just skin or drinks
Everything about her seemed in a drastic hurry to fade
From the blond hair just a shade lighter than her existence

Shadowing a tint around thought and upper body
Almost lost in the strong features, showing little
remorse for tonight
The only thing I could not find clear, were the dark eyes
Far from this room, in some distant place, that must be
cold
Creating the illusion of all the pain and sorrow,
Anger and confusion
That reason our skin tans and darkens then wrinkles
and ages
Collected in sight
Stuck behind black painted stain glass
Explaining her distant expressions, strength to be
Insightfully blind
When only some light came through but never seeing
the world in front of her
The room all but ignored her and just the opposite in
her mind
Modeling through the room until perching next to me
Pushing her hand through her hair and for a moment
Realizing
Not a single broken mind left its glass, to lose time in
her instead
Losing into reality and insult
The young girl
New for that duration of her walk
That simple presence from entrance till now
She
Was not luved
I could see the hurt as she ordered her drink
Windows almost leaking

If only she could cry drops of coal through black eyes.

Angelo: Staggering in and out of some lucid moment in time, he finds that place to stop the day and begin tonight.

Scene: The room was dark and reeked of hung memories. Staining the walls and floor with only a few framed times opposed fame found presence in public life. A small place with only a few black tables and two white benches at the oak bar. The person behind the bar hid under a top hat hiding the identity of what sex they were. Only providing curves and an Adams Apple as clues. Angelo sits left and Mariah Joe right.

Mariah Joe: You know when I was truly innocent and my eyes were blue, my heart could not have been a brighter shade of red. I had those who could get lost in my presence alone. My only desire was to spend time finding each other hidden behind curiously weak walls. I would spend hours in moments where the only thing needed was more time alone. There was this touch when I could feel the other person planting rose gardens around my heart with a path lined in orchids leading to my soul. Where they would sit and read my story to me when I felt lonely. Occasionally annotating their own lines just as a reminder they did care. Now, you can see right through my skin into my chest and the only thing you will see is a barren garden and a single bench with a book on it. A dried blood red hard cover that no longer has a title just a warn look and most of the pages missing.

Angelo: Thinking to himself, with slow breaths and a defeated drink. I could tell she began to sink into the last memory of a flower petal she held onto trying to picture the entire beauty of once. Not just a gifted flower but a plant that thrived off of happiness from being watered by companionship.

Angelo: If it means anything, I heard your presence when you walked into this place. I noticed your transparency to the world and how your moment was still living in the hopes of at least one person. Wondering why you walked through the room but not though any minds. As if you wanted to land, not thought of, but felt.

Mariah Joe: I wish I could believe that you could hear the music box playing in my head. That simple tone as each note places another stone on the slab on my chest. At best, there might be a vibration that could be felt from the anticipation of my burdened conclusion. But you're just a prisoned man, who spends his days dreaming of when he was a boy. When your lust was a place well lit by empowerment and feelings of immortality. Maybe as a youth you could hear my lullaby removed by that piece of puzzle you finally conformed. No, you my friend are as in shatters as I and your compass as broken. You say you can see how white my skin plays piano. We'll have you looked at yours? It's stained just the same, not with virgins but with filth and need. At least I still have my body's clarity.

Angelo: Then there are the whiskers to our kiss. To have had been in luv with you I would have had to find a dark place. A time where my body lingered in depth and artist suicide. Until the very notion, I want to live, was mute and the thought of release was time spent vulnerable to that novel in place of your organ. That very place I know you once hung pride, like a criminal so you may brag to others, proclaiming how your town was in the right and all others had to fall short of your towers or face fate. And if pride was lucky enough to be hung then any threat would just be burned and left with the pain of being an orphan to society. Wondering lost and in fear that the reason they are on the streets is because they murdered their parents and then had the grandparents pay for the funeral. Your right, I can't hear you and your music box. All I can hear are the church bells marking your funeral in my future and your conclusion. Sadly, I will not go to see the ground you will call home. As far as we go, I can see you already buried yourself.

Mariah Joe: A luver's history is a funny place to reside is it not? Just by the tone of your voice, I can hear the guilt and regret of your past echoing onto my sleeve.
Leaving this stain in a shape of a crying mime, as your face grows colder. It's not your choice to have emotions or not, you simply choose to ignore yourself entirely.

Like a drunk lost in the streets with only tunnel vision to provide support to an already lost cause. You sit there like you know what's best when what was best you lost a long time ago. This moment, full of reflection is in the arms of what you were. Proving, those bells you hear, are only of those that would have played at your wedding. If only you cared enough to live with forever. You're just as the rest in here really. Maybe luved a little more in the past but today loss is the reason you drink. Angelo, you once had a time when nothing mattered but your willingness to scratch a new record in attempts to prove individuality. The only thing stopping you now is your fascination with yesterday and its actors. All you have to do is let go.

Angelo: Orders another drink and finds his tongue caught.
Mariah Joe: When you were youthful you wrote life as it was a charm you could wear around your neck. Now it's just a birth mark you hid under conformity wishing you could have it removed. The adventure for the arts and humanity has just stopped and all you can do is wonder why you can't sleep? Look at yourself my luv. You have become framed and stuck on a wall with a simple title reading; lost. You can hide behind thick skin and words, but thoughts and your conscious can not be caged. Finickly robbing your soul so your material life has gain will only erase you as a person. Those gifts you had will grow dull and rust. That passion will become transparent and slowly fade. Childhood fantasies will seem like a good place to find

comfort when your mind drifts. Your personality will grow sick and start to cancer and eventually transform into a code represented only by numbers. If only you could have seen your creations that never had a chance to be born this might be clearer. Yet, those things uniquely yours are lost in some museum in a mind that has already rioted and burnt it down. The only thing surviving is your book. I can no longer protect it when I'm no longer desired.

Angelo: looks over to announce suspicion on how this stranger knows so much about him when all he turns to find is an empty seat. The next day Angelo finds himself past out on the steps of the Carnegie museum completely soaking wet from the rain. In his hand is a red book the color of dried blood with no title and mostly blank pages. Upon standing, he can see the dry spot on the steps where he laid. It looked as if it was his shadow pointing towards the grand building where a sign hung announcing, free admission.

A Night Spent In A Cave: A

My grandfather's clock explains everything to me, by grouping the hours of my life; No matter how each moment is consumed by my decisions, there is a chime to mark my constant. Yet as I stand here on the same streets with the surroundings never altered, I find that the people who I have, luved, moved on from my life. Not because of ugly altercations, lies or even hate. It seems as if my value to their wellbeing, is no longer what it used to be. As they grow through stages, evaluating time by their current place in the universe, not by a timely constant. To those who this might be true, I beg you to never forget, the chiming of your heart. Those moments were a number in your life that if altered may be forgotten. Sipping on my Cerveza, I find this to be an odd header for an Italian Menu, especially after the place I just came from and the walk that it took to bring me here. I order, then contemplate the day.

Dinners Contemplation: B

She stuck her pink nose up towards ancient streets, just as she walked away into her new self.
Never remembering young slits of time.
I can't help but wonder who has changed.
As I now arrange my thoughts through foreign alleys.
Was it youth or value that made our relationship?
I find little reason to watch her walk away for good allowing my feet to fall to the path of least resistance.

Right until my toes, stub onto wooden advertisement.
Monet inside.
Pondering if the sign was really that worn and chipped.
Or if my eyes still were glazed over.
Then my foot throbs from hitting the sign, bringing to
realization my hearts empty beat.
Thump.
Then nothing.
Thump.
Then nothing.
An empty space that once was filled with a person, in
desperate need to be occupied.
Finally following a group of people about to rebel
themselves through the side doors.
A simple effort to not pay the fee to get in.
Falling guilt free under the velvet ropes through carved
doors.
I find it's a church that has gone to rehab.
Rehabilitated in its stones and belief.
With every cross forced to be a star and star a moon.
The stain glass in revolt now, only spoke of long haired
people not saints.
Still for peace and luv, just not announcing one faith
over another.
Coming to the main hall I find a triangular room with
three doors.
In the middle, street signs pointed.
God's Anthropology Road.
Defiance Way.
People, Watching, Drive.

Still stumbling around weak from my organs revelation.
I timely followed the very next person.
Not really knowing what room I landed in, until I sat down.
As Avasa the bi-gender bi-sexual person in front of me explained to her holy book.
Defiance was hard and people watching really made me wonder their stories.
I hope God's Anthropology gives me answers.
Till this day I wonder if their book ever answered back.
Regardless, I quickly became distracted by the far wall.
On the bottom were very small books, titled, Wealth, Power, Economics.
With my eyes only able to follow the colorful books, I realized that they were getting bigger.
To the point at the top holding up the ceiling, sat 6 foot tall giants, boldly titled.
Why part one, ? Why part two? And, what's it all about, part three?
Completely fascinated on how to, they ever managed to pull one out and read it.
Not fearing they would all fall and be crushed, was probably why I missed the speech completely.
As the applause broke my focus.
Just to find Avasa, floating in a pool of nonalcoholic wine, with a gold candle on her back.
I thought it best to gather my respects and finish finding Monet.
After that, my epiphany on luv had turned into confusion and that's where I existed.

Some place made of carved stone, that one could get lost in, forever, like a mind or generation.
Luckily my hurt toe and half a heart guided me to the visitor's desk.
A plaque read Zephyr.
Better explained as an elder woman behind a bamboo desk and wearing what looked like black scrubs.
I stared at her for what seemed like hours until she said, "excuse me"
Yes, that's what I should have said but she said it to herself for me.
Then she went on…
Can you help me find the famous painting?
Again, that's probably what I would have asked, if not to question why she had my voice.
Just go down until you can't go down any further, then turn left.
It's right behind the broken silver light fixture.
Exhausted from my minds intrusion, but content in the answer, I went to say thank you, when;
"Do you mind if we go with him?"
This voice from behind me ask.
Zephyr answers, "well, it's really not up to me, so I can't say"
Regardless, I guess my look said ok, so mother and daughter chained themselves to my heal.
Down the mossy stairs around the uneven bends past filth and age, until finally I find it.
The 6x6 painting of the bearded man stuck behind the broken fixture…
Just as promised.

Not really impressed or in belief it was really a Monet. I find a wall to lean on.
Still looking at the painting thinking; It's a paint by numbers!
I can't help but watch my imagination cry, and take pictures over the infamous art.
Just before the daughter cracked the corner of the painting off and sticks it on her charm bracelet.
As if that was not shock enough, the mother went up and licked the other side.
Turning and smiling at me proclaiming it's all in one's own taste.
Amused and no longer thinking of why I came here, I thought it best to move on.
After all, I feared, if I stayed, there would be nothing left of an example for others to see.
Getting some space between myself and the others, I find flesh on auto pilot.
Walking right into the wall just before it rotates, I land on entirely new steps.
Glad to be alone breathing deeply to calm myself down, I hear a painted tongue say, he went this way.
And there, they were right behind me again.
Walking on further and further down, way below the Monet and past the normal decent, I hit the end...
Just an empty room with forgotten junk and useless items for past decoration.
I go to turn around when I found the ladies daughter breaking the lock to a set of oak doors.
Smiling and saying, "If it was easy, they would not lock it"

The opening was only 3 feet tall and looked like a closet for more stuff.

She crawled in past the dust and support beams just far enough into the shadows. I lost sight of her

All I could do is listen to the shuffling of the junk and the occasional discontent voice.

Seems like she had been her before and had placed something in that hole along with the others.

Finally appearing in the light and landing softly in front of me, she kneeled.

Here you go, holding out two legs from a forgotten table and an old guitar.

I heard you could use some support to stand on and a beat in your heart.

I found my way out of that thought and discovered the day, just as I left it. Standing there with my back turned watching my friend walk away out of the car mirror with no idea if the girl really knew, or was she just making a joke. Entering the restaurant, I'm sitting by the window with a view of the church, allowing my mind to slip away.

A Rose Garden Called; A Child's Grave

Scene: I got up in a room with a cold pulse, only lit by the bleached light on the far wall. Dusty stains hung on the egg shell confinement, well faded from the original brilliance. Still, I could see the light casted from the window edging her figure upon the abstract hill. She was young in thought then, as was our mistakes. Regardless, the touch of our now aged hands still felt warm, if only between us and our history. I could tell the sky, hung by the light, acting as clouds, projecting over my subconscious painted and framed. My drugged eyes, swaggering to the tired hour, as if my mind was ready to start its nightly game. A voice, from a lifeless body, echoed from the memory.

Eden: The colors in this painting once knew who I was, if only in interpretations to my physical acts. It's no longer who I pretend to be in the sight of strangers. It deserves to be added to a more private collection of lies not hung in your view. When all is left is white for me, I beg you to take it down.

Jesse: He takes a deep breath and a slight chill runs over his nerves

Eden: This flesh you sleep with will one day fade; leaving only the scenery as this creations focus. Never blaming the lack of details on the earth, as the light

128

bleeds the page blank. Providing only wonder to the passerby to what's missing from the outlined soul.

Jesse: Never before has Eden said this or has Jesse seen the picture so dark.

Eden: My view should be of my garden where my kids are all played out in peace and finding blossom with each passing season. Not to say our luv was not true in the moments in life but these sheets have only imprisoned our existence in a single action and obsession. Knowing very well this would end, in one, not three.

Jesse: But you are not some inspiration that lies upon my body and plays my strings to produce a tune any more than a barren and mute mother. It's the very way you move through my body that gives my hand the courage to dance the way it does, across your presence and canvas alike. Every moment your beauty screams out to be ugly and harsh, I find grace in your mind and tainted words that excite my life. The further from reality you slip away, the more understanding of my expressions, the world will have. For what makes insanity, not defined as luv, but the definition strongly opinioned people verbalize.

Eden: Tossing, showing only back

As the night faded, concentration on the painting neglected the two repeated the conversation in their head.

Eden: It's important that I am the only one who knows the reason you express only me. Society may never find out why my eyes are sorrowed, my skin discolored. Or the explanation my presence was soft then later painful. For let them believe is was for the passion and hurt from our unborn family. They will not understand my life's purpose, planting the cemetery of kids so they may have a mother. I understand only my death will be your great tragic loss, fueling this madness you not seek but embrace. Yet, please never speak of the perfectly buried truth. Don't ever take that away from me.

Jesse: Dead silent

Eden: I want you to live and prove falsely that we luved and only had moral secrets. Cover up our true embrace, for life and those born without parents. Never point to our immaterial belongings but only to those things people can see. Paint gardens full of trees and roses not gravestones and dirt.

Jesse: And for you?

Eden: Plant me with the family, when the season is right. Watering only from your left hand, dream, perfectly inspired, with newspaper passion. Never from yourself show the true source of fear and rage. I know you will soon own your actions and motivations. If you truly understand my soul, you will let anger go, along with the misunderstanding of how I must transform now, if not then. If this part we share continues to weave on, the created will never happen. Time will only bring content and if not my sorrow then the stale air and society will kill you.

Long pause

Jesse: Not in your eyes or posture will people know of how we held hands in this time. I will simply paint a rose, pinned to our shirts over our hearts, symbolizing your motherhood and nothing more. For the rest of it will be only a decoy to how we lived, the best way we knew how, if only stepping over humanities norm.

Eden: Rolls over, woken by Jesse. In a groggy conscious mind she ask,

"Do you think it's going to rain?"

Jesse: "Yeah, I think so, I can feel the pressure in my head, the thunder off the wall

Eden: "That's good the flowers could use it"

Jesse: Kissing Eden and wrapping his body around hers, the storm rolls in....

End:

Jesse thinks about everything Eden said in her sleep
and realizes that maybe she should take down some of
the paintings. After all, people might not see how hard
she worked to fertilize the land. If they knew why the
plants are so lush, the grace might be lost. With that the
two fall asleep.

Starry Night

The Scene:

Joe sits in front of a wall on a statistically placed wooden bench in a typical museum setting. The walls are white and plain, as not to distract, the lighting ideal. An almost perfect place for a high school field trip. Deborah, a shy girl, with pop bottle glasses, bright red hair and a hole in her jeans, hesitantly walks across the room and sits next to Joe.

Deborah: In a quiet voice, "Hey Joe"

Joe: Silence

Deborah: "Um, are you ok"

Joe: Silence

Deborah: "Please talk to me"

Joe: Sighs, "I'm ok, just leave me alone"

Deborah: "Not until you tell me why you're crying"

Joe: Silence

Deborah: "Is it the painting? You know this is my favorite painting by Van Gogh? I think it's because I enjoy starry nights in general, especially if it's summer and..."

Joe: "Please just go away!"

Deborah: Taking a deep breath and hesitating; "This painting reminds me when I spent the weekend at my grandparents farm and my grandpa would spin me around the back yard by my arms and we both would fall over from being so dizzy and lay on our backs looking into the starry night trying to find the big dipper and then...."

Joe: "Do you ever shut up? Just stop, ok?, I don't care about all the stupid paintings!"

Silence....

Deborah: "You don't have to be mean Joe, I was just trying to cheer you up"

Joe: "I just hate museums, it's nothing you did"

Deborah: Jumps off the bench hands in the air and proclaims

"What!, How can you hate museums? There is so much history and culture, not to mention all the passion and emotion and even all that aside, there is so much color and energy in each individual piece, how could you hate art?"

Teacher: "Deb, inside voices"

Joe: "Physical art holds no justice to me"

Deborah: "What!?, No justice!? How can you sit here on this bench the entire trip, staring at my favorite painting in the world! Then tell me you hate it!? And not just Starry Night, but all the art in this entire museum?!!

Teacher: "Deborah please, inside voices!"

Deborah: Whispering, "I just think you're ignorant to real beauty"

Joe: "No, just blind to it"
Deborah: "HA! Yea, you can say that again!. You would not know true beauty if it walked up and hit you in the face!

Teacher: "Deborah, I'm not going to tell you again!

Deborah: Ugh, sits back down next to Joe.

Joe: "Your right you know, true beauty could be sitting next to me, silent as glass, flowing and I would never know"

Deborah: "And to think, my mom was right about boys"

Joe: "I don't think you understand"

Joe: Sliding his shades off and looking towards Deborah.

Deborah: Fear and sadness comes over her face, "You're really blind…"

Joe: "Yea, and not just physical"

Deborah: "I'm so sorry Joe, you probably think I'm a bitch. I just thought you wore those rose colored shades to be cool and see the world in a better shade, not to hide your eyes"

Joe: "Well, you thought wrong"

Deborah: Silence

Joe: "Now you know why I was just sitting here and not perusing all the wonderful nothingness"

Deborah: Silence

Joe: "To you, this may be a pool of inspiring brush strokes and design, but for me, it's an orchestra of shoes echoing off the marble floor. With an occasion vocal whispering how beautiful everything is, like the

136

fat lady with the cotton shoes who drags her feet! Or the bimbo with high hills who wants to drag all the attention off the art and onto her or the school of sneakers from being wet cause of the rain! Yea, I just love this Fucking place!

Teacher: "Inside voices Joe and watch your language!"

Deborah: Silence

Joe: All this place reminds me of is the summer I spent in the hospital after my first eye surgery and my eyes were all wrapped up so I could not see a thing, all I could do is sit and listen to the shoes walk up and down the hallway.

Deborah: Silence

Joe: Silence

Joe: "I'm sorry for freaking out on you"

Deborah: Silence

Joe: "Say something"

Deborah: "Something"

Joe: "If anything, at least describe this painting to me..."

Deborah: Leans over and kisses Joe, "Did you see it, the Starry Night?"

Joe: Red in the face and stuttering, "Is that what it really looks like?"

Deborah: Smiling, "yup, that's exactly what the painting looks like"

Joe: "The colors really that bright?"

Deborah: "Yes"

Joe: "The emotion that deep?"

Deborah: "Yes"

Joe: "And the beauty so breath taking?"

Deborah: Blushing, "that's up to the beholder"

Joe: "Kiss me again"

End Scene:
Joe and Deborah sitting on a statistically placed bench, with ideal lighting facing a blank wall, not to distract.

Notes:

Draw Here:

Write Your Own Revolt Here:

18134118R00089

Made in the USA
Charleston, SC
18 March 2013